In a Tropical Rain Forest

by Katherine Scraper

Table of Contents

I need to know these words.

canopy

emergent layer

equator

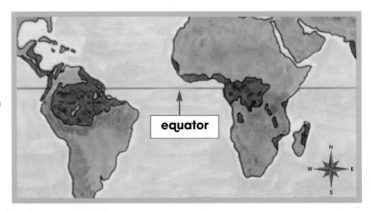

equator

forest floor

rain forest

understory

3

What Is a Tropical Rain Forest?

A tropical **rain forest** is a habitat.
This habitat is near the **equator**.
A tropical rain forest is very warm
and very wet.

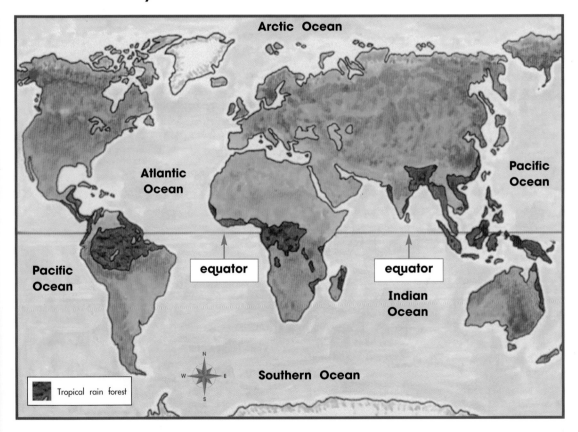

A tropical rain forest has many different types of animals. A rain forest has different types of plants, too.

▲ A tropical rain forest can get 400 inches (1,000 centimeters) of rain each year.

A tropical rain forest has four layers, or parts. The first layer is the **forest floor**. The forest floor is dark.

The second layer is the **understory**. The understory has some sunlight.

Most treetops are in the third layer, the **canopy**. The canopy has more sunlight than the understory.

The tallest treetops are in the fourth layer, the **emergent layer**.

emergent layer

canopy

understory

forest floor

What Animals Live in a Tropical Rain Forest?

Many animals live in a tropical rain forest. Different animals live in each layer. Some insects have nests on the forest floor. Some animals eat plants from the forest floor.

▲ leaf-cutting ants

▼ tapir

Some animals move between the forest floor and the understory. Other animals live mostly in the understory.

◀ A red-eyed tree frog eats insects in the understory.

▲ Jaguars rest or hide in the understory.

The canopy has the most animals. You can see small animals like butterflies and bats. You can see large animals like sloths.

◀ sloth

▲ fruit bats

butterfly ▶

The emergent layer is home to many birds. The birds have nests in the branches.

▲ toucan

▲ macaw

▲ parrot

▲ harpy eagle

What Plants Live in a Tropical Rain Forest?

Many plants live in a tropical rain forest.
Woody vines grow from the forest floor.
The vines climb the trees to reach sunlight.

▲ Some vines climb more than one tree.

Many fruits grow in the canopy. The canopy and emergent layer are also homes for air plants. Air plants do not need soil. They can live on the branches.

◄ The orchid is a beautiful air plant.

▲ Bananas grow in a tropical rain forest.

Why Are Tropical Rain Forests in Danger?

Our tropical rain forests are getting smaller. People cut down the trees. People use the trees for wood.

▲ People cut trees to get wood.

People use the land in other ways, too. People plant crops on the land. People build things on the land. People let farm animals eat, or graze, on the land.

Now people are making laws. The laws will help protect the tropical rain forests. The laws protect the plants and animals.

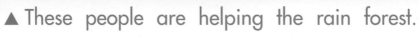

▲ These people are helping the rain forest.